Old Age Isn't for Sissies

Compliments of:

TRIBUNE
MEDIA SERVICES
www.tms.tribune.com

For Lola Rayder, World War II veteran and proud member of the "Greatest Generation."

Old Age Isn't for Sissies

A Lola Collection

Steve Dickenson and Todd Clark

**Andrews McMeel
Publishing**

Kansas City

Lola is syndicated worldwide by Tribune Media Services, Inc.

www.comicspage.com

Old Age Isn't for Sissies copyright © 2001 Tribune Media Services, Inc.
All rights reserved. Printed in the United States of America. No part of this book may be used or reproduced in any manner whatsoever without written permission except in the case of reprints in the context of reviews. For information, write Andrews McMeel Publishing, an Andrews McMeel Universal company, 4520 Main Street, Kansas City, Missouri 64111.

ISBN: 0-7407-1842-8

02 03 04 05 BAH 10 9 8 7 6 5 4 3 2

Library of Congress Catalog Card Number: 2001086435

——— ATTENTION: SCHOOLS AND BUSINESSES ———

Andrews McMeel books are available at quantity discounts with bulk purchase for educational, business, or sales promotional use. For information, please write to: Special Sales Department, Andrews McMeel Publishing, 4520 Main Street, Kansas City, Missouri 64111.

WITH DAD GONE NOW, I'D BE MORE COMFORTABLE WITH YOU LIVING HERE, MOM.

BESIDES, WOULDN'T YOUR CONDO HAVE TOO MANY MEMORIES?

4/19

YOU'RE RIGHT, SON. I SHOULD PUT THOSE MEMORIES OF CENTRAL AIR, A POOL, AND A HOT TUB BEHIND ME.

DICKENSON & CLARK

BOY, WHAT A TOUGH DAY AT WORK.

I LIVED THROUGH THE DEPRESSION AND A WORLD WAR. SO TELL ME, WHAT WAS SO TOUGH ABOUT **YOUR** DAY?

4/20
DICKENSON & CLARK

WELL, THE COPIER WAS JAMMED FOR QUITE A WHILE.

OOH. ANY SURVIVORS?

THANKS FOR COMING TO EAT LUNCH WITH ME AT SCHOOL, GRAMMA!

I WOULDN'T HAVE MISSED GRANDPARENTS DAY FOR ANYTHING, SAMMY.

SLURKKK

IT ISN'T ALLOWED.

SHOULDN'T WE SAY GRACE FIRST?

4/21

CAN WE SACRIFICE SOMETHING?

DICKENSON & CLARK

24

33

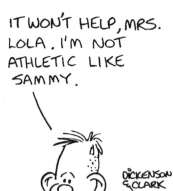

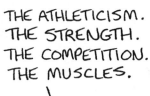

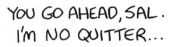

SAMMY SURE IS GROWING, THE LITTLE CUSS HAS GONE THROUGH TWO SIZES IN THE PAST SIX MONTHS...

AND THAT SON OF YOURS HAS FINALLY STAYED AT A JOB LONGER THAN THREE WEEKS, AND DON'T GET ME STARTED ON AMY.

SEE YOU TOMORROW, CRAWFORD.

I DIDN'T LET HIM GET A WORD IN EDGEWISE WHEN HE WAS ALIVE-I'M NOT ABOUT TO START NOW.

THAT'S FOR SURE

CRAWFORD

11/29

HOW LONG WERE YOU AND CRAWFORD MARRIED, LOLA?

55 YEARS, SAL.

AND THEY WERE FANTASTIC... ALL EXCEPT FOR THE ROMANCE.

CRAWFORD'S IDEA OF A HOT DATE WAS GRABBING A TWELVE-PACK AND WATCHING THE BUG ZAPPER.

11/30

I PREFER THE PARK AFTER HOURS, SALLY...

THE PANHANDLERS AREN'T IN YOUR FACE.

THANKS, LADIES!

NIGHT DEPOSITS

12/1